*REE*cipe
For Success

A COOKBOOK WITH A RECIPE FOR LIFE

By Lareesa Fonville

Dedicated in Loving Memory

to

My father, Elder Lynwood E. Fonville, Sr.
(1949-2005)
For teaching me how to persevere

My grandmothers, Marjorie L. Fonville (1928-1988)
and Mary S. Branch (1925-2008)
For teaching me the power of prayer

My grandfather, Herbert L. Branch (1925-1998)
For teaching me the value of hard work

Table of Contents

Acknowledgments

First and foremost, I would like to thank God. Without Him, I am nothing. He is everything to me. In Him I live, move, and have my being.

To my mother, Elder Katrina B. Fonville, words cannot express how much I love, cherish, and appreciate you. THANK YOU for your unconditional love, support, and for giving me a gift that will never go out style, never fade, or go away. You gave me Jesus. You not only taught me about Christ, you showed Him to me in your daily walk. Thank you, M.

A big thank you to everyone who has supported and encouraged me, not only in the creation of this book, but also in my many other endeavors. I love you all!

From the Author

Dear Reader,

Thank you for taking the time to read "REEcipe For Success." I'm glad you're here. Really, I am. But, I must tell you that this book wasn't started for you. It was started for me. I know that might sound a little crazy, but it's true. There are thousands of books out here on this very subject. I could've very well chosen to read one of them. But, I needed more. I needed to remind *myself* to do the daily activities required not only to be successful, but to *remain successful*.

So, yes. This book was started for me, but it was published for YOU. It is my prayer that you learn something within these pages that will expand your mind, grow your business, and improve your life. No matter your current situation, today in this very moment, I want you to know that SUCCESS – whatever that means to you – is attainable. But, that success is solely up to you.

God bless you,
Lareesa

Introduction

· A Blue Book and a Green Box ·

As a child, I grew up thinking my grandmothers were from two different worlds. But, looking back now, it seems they had more similarities than differences. In fact, they had a lot in common. They were women of great faith, courage, hardworking, had servant hearts, treasured their families, and they both loved to cook.

Marjorie Fonville, my father's mother, was born in Kinston, North Carolina in 1928. She was the daughter of a Sharecropper.

Mary Sydnor Branch, my mother's mother, was born in Richmond, Virginia in 1925. She was the daughter of a Laborer.

Both ladies grew up in homes where they witnessed hard work firsthand. They knew from birth that if they wanted anything out of this life, they had to work for it. And, work they did.

They were successful wives, mothers, aunts, cousins, and friends. In my eyes, they achieved greatness, and showed me I could do the same. Their lives spoke volumes and even if I tried, I couldn't recount the many stories from the lives they touched.

I grew up enjoying the love that flowed through their kitchens. Food wasn't just food in their homes. It was pure love. From the smells to the tastes, to the smiles that were exchanged. Pure love.

We said grace over every meal, truly thankful to God for providing our needs. Praying before a meal wasn't a habit. It was real, from the heart, and always followed by a scripture. Although, I must admit my brothers and I hurried to see who could say, "Jesus wept" first. Those were the good, old days and it makes me smile now to think about it. With two competitive brothers, I usually lost, so my favorite scripture became, "Greater is He that is in you (me), than he that is in the world."

I still carry that scripture around with me, 1 John 4:4. It reminds me that God is greater than any problem I could ever face. Nothing in this world is greater than Him and because He is in me, I can face and overcome anything.

Both of my grandmothers knew the Lord and with Him, they overcame many obstacles. I watched them tarry and have unshakeable faith. I admired their strength, tenacity, and courage... and, I believe every ounce of who they were poured out into their meals. I know it might sound crazy, but...

Have you ever eaten something and it tasted like love? Well, that's what eating anything made by my grandmothers tasted like. Oh how I miss them.

When Grandma Fonville passed away, a scholarship fund was started and we sold cookbooks with a collection of family/friends to help raise funds. I still have that blue book.

When Granny (Grandmother Branch) passed away, we found recipe after recipe. Some torn out of magazines, some typed neatly on index cards, others scribbled in pencil just barely readable. I still have that green recipe box. She traded these recipes with neighbors, friends, and church members. She was happy to oblige anyone requesting how to prepare one of her meals.

In fact, both of them were very giving. Most people try to keep things to themselves. I admired them for their spirit of sharing. They lived by the rule, "When you learn, teach. When you get, give." I think that's why I am willing to freely share with others today.

Even though I'm focusing on their culinary skills, they were always willing to help anyone in need... in and out the kitchen.

Within these pages, I will share with you some things I've learned from them, and others, along the way.

But, first, let's make this perfectly clear. I'm no expert on success. I'm out here just like you trying to win at this thing called life.

I, also, seldom use recipes as intended. I usually just look at the directions, and make the dish my own. I'm quick to put in a pinch of this and a dash of that. So, that's what I want you to do. I want you to read the information provided in this book and *make it your own.* Success is unique, just like you.

You know, I've read countless books on personal development and the one thing each of them have in common is this: **Success is up to you.**

You are the catalyst. You are the key. You are the engine. You are the fuel. You!

You can dream as much as you want. You can believe as much as you want. You can even spend every waking moment in prayer. But, nothing will happen unless YOU start moving towards the success you seek.

To do that, you must have a plan. A clear, concise plan. A blueprint for your ultimate success. Yes, you must move, but you need to first know where you are going, why you're going, and how you're going to get there. So, if you're ready to finally have the success you've been dreaming of, follow this REEcipe.

What is Success?

· noun | suc·cess | \sək-'ses\ ·

Merriam Webster defines success as:

- the fact of getting or achieving wealth, respect, or fame
- the correct or desired result of an attempt
- someone or something that is successful: a person or thing that succeeds

But...

What does success mean to you? Go ahead, take a second to jot it down.

_____

_____

_____

_____

_____

_____

_____

_____

_____

_____

_____

_____

_____

_____

_____

_____

_____

_____

_____

_____

_____

_____

_____

_____

_____

_____

_____

If you're not sure, it's ok. Success is different for everyone. But, know that only you can define what it means for you.

That's really the purpose of this book. To help you answer this question. Everything else in this book is to encourage you to achieve it. To me, success is more about meaningful relationships and self-fulfillment. Not material things, wealth, and fame. But, whatever it means to you, this book will help you prepare, attain, and lead a healthy, fulfilled, successful life.

Are you ready?

We are going to jump right in. But, first, let's make sure we have everything we need.

Ingredients:

- 1 VISION
- 3 ¼ cups all-purpose WHY
- 5 large FOCUS
- 2 tablespoons BELIEF (100%)
- 1 pinch of FAITH (mustard seed size)
- 1 ½ teaspoon NEVER GIVE UP extract
- 3 cups SERVICE TO OTHERS
- 1 ½ cup ACTION
- 4 DISCIPLINE
- 1 dash CONSISTENCY
- Garnish: POSITIVITY

Directions:

1. Preheat your **Faith** to 350°. Beat *fear* at high speed with a heavy-duty **Vision** mixer until **Belief** occurs. Gradually add **Action**; beat at medium speed 3 to 5 minutes or until **Dedicated** and **Consistent**. **Remove Bad Seeds** and add 4 **Focus**, 1 at a time, beating just until **Vision** becomes clearer. After each addition, remember your **Why**. Stir in **Positivity** zest and **Discipline** extracts.

2. Add more **Action** to mixture, alternately with remaining **Focus**, beginning and ending with your

Why. Beat at low speed until blended. Pour **Dreams** into a greased and floured *limitless* pan.

3. Bake at 350° for as long as it takes for your **Why** to become reality. Cool away from negative people.

4. Spoon **Helping Others** Glaze over warm or room temperature. Top **Success** with **Thankfulness** and **Giving Back**.

The recipe seems simple enough, right? But, being successful isn't as easy as I've just made it seem. **Success is a dish that only you can create** and just like any dish, **you are responsible for the outcome**.

There needs to be some preparation and each ingredient needs to be right before adding it to the mix. So, let's get to it!

Ingredient #1

·Write the Vision·

What do you want? I mean, really, really want? Do you want to get out of debt? Do you want to provide for your family? What are your goals? If you are without goals, you're like a ship without a destination. Just drifting through life. Goals provide a sense of direction, so let's chart the course by writing them down now.

_____

_____

_____

_____

_____

_____

_____

_____

_____

_____

_____

_____

_____

_____

_____

_____

_____

_____

_____

_____

_____

_____

_____

_____

_____

_____

_____

I hope you took the time to write down your goals. If you were thinking of going back to it later, stop. **Do it now**. Don't procrastinate. Successful people don't procrastinate and since I know you know what you want, get it out of your head and onto paper. Now.

Did you know that writing down your goals increases the odds of you achieving them? It's true! Don't ask me to prove it with charts and graphs, just trust me on this one. It's helped me tremendously. Quite frankly, I really don't see how people go through life without bothering to write down their goals. The Bible actually tells us to do so.

"And the LORD answered me, and said, Write the vision, and make *it* plain upon tables, that he may run that readeth it." – Habakkuk 2:2 KJV

It doesn't get much clearer than that. I'm not just telling you to write your goals down. God himself is telling you to write them down, clearly, so you can win.

Now, I know I didn't give you much space to write on, but there is more space in the back of this book. You're going to need it because **I want you to write down every goal: personal, professional, and physical.**

What do you want? Think about it. Even if you want something that you have no idea how it's going to happen, write it down! Do you have a health goal? Weight loss goal? Exercise goal? Career goal? Family goal? Faith goal?

"Every great dream begins with a dreamer. Always remember, you have within you the strength, the patience, and the passion to reach for the stars to change the world." - Harriet Tubman

Get specific. I mean, super specific and set a time limit for you to accomplish them. This is not the time to be vague about what you want. Be clear and precise. I want you take a second, close your eyes, and visualize what you want. See it happening. What will you feel like? What will you be wearing? Who will be with you? Go ahead, dream... I'll wait.

Dreaming in Progress

Welcome back! Could you see it? Could you feel it? Could you even smell it? Yes, even smell it! I know you think I'm crazy by now, and I've got to admit, I am. I'm crazy enough to believe that I'm going to succeed and if you want to be successful, you've got to be crazy about your dreams, too!

Now that us crazy folks have written down our goals, we need to put our goals somewhere we can see them. You don't have to do this part right now. But, I want you to *commit* to putting your goals somewhere you can see them *daily*. Even if that means neatly rewriting them or turning them into a visually appealing vision board. I have my goals on the wall in my bedroom and look at them every day. It helps to remind me to do the things daily that will bring me closer to attaining my goals and to say no to the things that will deter me from them.

Congratulations on preparing your first ingredient! Now, let's keep going.

Ingredient #2

· What is your WHY? ·

Why are you doing this? The goals you wrote down for ingredient #1, why do you want them? What will happen when you've accomplished your goals? Who will benefit from your dream becoming reality? Your children? Your spouse? Your church? Your community? Dig deep. Why are you doing this? Why? Have you ever thought about it before? I mean, really thought about it? You must know this to truly win. If you don't, you will fall prey to distractions, which ultimately lead to failure.

> **"He who has a why can endure any how."**
> **-Frederick Nietzsche**

Knowing your why is so very important. I probably should've made this ingredient #1. But, I've learned over the years that people don't like to dig deep. Not right away at least. So, I wanted you to get your goals down first. To think about the life you want to actually live. Your WHY is going to allow you to figure out HOW to achieve those goals.

This is an *unavoidable* step, by the way. Only when you know your why will you have the courage to take the necessary risks involved to be successful. Your why is going to help you stay motivated when you feel like giving up. You *will* feel like giving up. You *will* want to quit. Many times. Many, many times. **But, your why won't let you.** That's why you can't skip this step. The process is the process, and you my friend, have to go through the process.

"The process is the process and you can't skip the process."

So, how do you find your why? Good question. It wasn't easy for me at first. I started with surface answers just to get something on paper. But, I knew it wasn't my real why because it didn't make me cry. Your why will move you to tears. Every person's why is different and despite what others may want you to believe, there are no right or wrong answers. Your why is your why. But, it has to move you. Because if your why doesn't move you, it won't move your dreams. You'll just be someone with big dreams, stuck, mediocre... and, that's not you. How do I know that? You wouldn't be reading a book like this one if you were average and didn't want more out of your life.

"If your why doesn't move you, it won't move your dreams."

In a second, I'm going to ask you to write down your why. I just want you to get something down on paper. Don't stress about it. Here are some more questions to help you:

What is it that you can contribute to the world? What do you value most? What do you care about? What makes you, YOU? What makes you get out of bed in the morning? What makes you come alive? Feel alive? What inspires you? What drives you? What are you passionate about? Think outside of yourself. Where can you add value? If you didn't become successful, who would you be letting down? Who will you make proud by becoming successful?

I know these are tough questions to think about. I'm just trying to get you to really think. Now, take some time and write down your WHY.

_____

_____

_____

_____

_____

_____

_____

_____

_____

_____

_____

_____

_____

_____

_____

_____

_____

_____

_____

_____

_____

_____

_____

I'm glad you took the time to do that. Know that your why will change and grow with you over time. Remember I said, there is no right or wrong. We start where we start. So, with that being said, even if you also started with a surface answer like I did in the beginning, it's ok, for now. You'll soon find out, like I did, that your real why isn't a material thing. Money alone can't buy a why. It's deeper than a new house and it will take you further than a new car.

Your why is a very special ingredient. It does many things. It adds a lot of sustenance to your dish. It will hold you over until you get to your next meal. It will also keep you hungry for more. But, it also does something else.

Every good, shareable recipe has measurements. Exact measurements. If the recipe calls for 1 ½ cup of flour and you just put in ½ cup, most likely you won't like the results of your dish. So, we need to get our measurements right.

You need to measure your life. I know this sounds weird, but try to follow me. Your WHY is going to be your measuring tool. *You are going to decide what your why is and then align your life to your why.* Make sense? In order to be successful, every aspect of your life needs to line up with your why. That's living with purpose, ON PURPOSE!

Your WHY is the greater purpose. It's WHY you do what you do… and, it fuels the HOW. Knowing this will stretch you in unimaginable ways. It will challenge who you thought you were. It will inspire you to great lengths. It will light a fire in your belly that will radiate through anything. YOUR WHY. It's power. Find your power. Find your why. Once you find it, help others find theirs too.

Ingredient #3

· Mix in Faith ·

We are not only going to cook with our faith, but we are also throwing faith into the mix!

I don't know what you believe. But, I do know this: You must believe that its possible. But, not *just* that its possible. That it is possible *for* YOU.

Do you think others are more deserving of success than you are? That's a question you need to ask yourself. Do you? I'm asking you this question because, if you don't feel deserving, you'll find a way not to allow yourself to have whatever it is you want out of life. You'll sabotage yourself. I've been there, many times. Because of unbelief, you'll mess something up, not follow through, or retreat completely from the process. It can be a vicious cycle of self-sabotage until we believe we are deserving. I want you to know, it is possible for you. Success is possible for you!

I don't know what caused you to begin feeling this way. Everybody is different. It could've stemmed from something that happened in childhood, a relationship, loss, or other negative experience. Whatever it was, you're getting unstuck today.

Repeat after me, "I am worthy of success." Say it out loud. I don't care who is around you. Say it out loud. You not only need to say it; you need to hear it. From yourself.

Say it until you believe it. Successful people believe they deserve success, whereas unsuccessful people do not. If you have any beliefs that support you're not deserving of success, it *will* hold you back from creating the success you want in your life. This is also an important ingredient. One of the most important.

Have faith in yourself. Success won't work if you don't. Nothing will work if you don't. Are you determined to fail? I don't think so, because if you were, you wouldn't be reading this book.

Lack of belief in yourself will limit you no matter how great your skillset is, how awesome your ideas are, or how many opportunities that come your way.

Fear and faith can't operate at the same time. Either you are going to have faith that it will work or you're going to be scared to reach your potential. The choice is yours and yours alone. Nobody can walk this journey out for you. Nobody can cook this dish for you and you can't skip this ingredient either. You can try, but you'll be right back where you started if you do.

Instead of searching for reasons why it won't work, come up with reasons why it will.

"Successful people have fear, successful people have doubts, and successful people have worries. They just don't let these feelings stop them." --T. Harv Eker

We all deal with feelings of doubt and failure, but we have to trust that when we move forward anyway, we'll win.

When I started my network marketing business, I was at a very low point in my life. I was in a failing marriage, my beauty school and salon recently closed, years later I was still mourning the death of my father, I was morbidly obese, and I was stuck. Because I came in with an independent mindset, initially I was left to figure things out on my own. But, I trusted that it HAD to work for me. I trusted that I would figure it out. I trusted that God would place the right people in my life to help me, and He did!

My network marketing career has allowed me to touch hundreds of lives. It helped me create an income more than what I was making. It has allowed me to travel and experience things I'd once only dreamed of. It gave me the freedom to enjoy life, to do what I want, when I want, and with whom I want.

What if I hadn't had faith? I'd still be stuck. I believe it's possible to raise the bar on our lives. I believe we shouldn't accept ourselves as average. I believe that success is within us, we just have to tap into the part of ourselves that believes it is. Once we do that, it will radiate into whatever area we choose.

"Our deepest fear is not that we are inadequate. Our deepest fear is that we are powerful beyond measure. It is our light, not our darkness, that most frightens us. We ask ourselves, 'Who am I to be brilliant, gorgeous, talented, fabulous?' Actually, who are you not to be?" --Marianne Williamson

Who are you not to be? Why not you and why not now?

I know I've talked about faith and belief like they are the same thing. They aren't, but they do go hand in hand. That's why I use them interchangeably. You can have one without the other, but its futile.

You can believe something all day long, but faith is taking the next step. Belief is an opinion of judgement in which a person is persuaded. Faith is the *complete* trust or confidence in someone or something.

Belief is aiming to do something; Faith is pulling the trigger!

I get it, sometimes it's just hard to have faith. Especially when life throws stumbling block after stumbling block. If it were easy, everybody would be doing it. But, walking things out with nothing but faith is HARD. But, what are you going to do? Stay down? No. No way. That's not you. So, you must hold on. You know what the good thing is? You don't even need to have a lot of faith. The Bible tells us that if we just somehow gather up faith as a mustard seed, we can move mountains. Do you know how small a mustard seed is? A mustard seed is smaller than any other seed. One grain is 1 or 2 millimeters in size. That's about the size of the tip of a sharpened pencil. That's super tiny. When mustard seeds are planted, they grow up to become trees that are larger than all other plants; producing large branches for birds to nest in.

Now, I'm not a Bible scholar. But, I recall when the disciples asked Jesus to increase their faith, He said:

"Because of your unbelief; for assuredly, I say to you, if you have faith as a mustard seed, you will say to this mountain, 'Move from here to there,' and it will move; and nothing will be impossible for you. — *Matthew 17:20 (NKJV)*

Even as I'm writing these words, this is blessing me. To think, Jesus could've instantly increased the disciple's faith. After all, this was Jesus! A man who could heal the sick and raise the dead!

But, Jesus told them they didn't need a huge amount of faith. That all they needed was to have faith as a mustard seed.

Yet, I don't believe He was only talking about size. I believe He was talking about using it as you would a mustard seed. What do you do with a mustard seed? You plant it! You sow it! So, it will grow!

How do we sow (grow) our faith? When you plant a seed, you put it somewhere. Usually that place is in soil. We need to put our faith somewhere, too. But where, you ask? In God's hands! What better place is there for us to put our faith? Give God your love, time, finances, whatever it is that you have. Our giving reflects our trust in God and the moment we ask God for something and plant our seed of faith, we should expect that the answer is on its way... because it is! There isn't a gardener out here that plants something and doesn't expect it to grow. That's the purpose of the planting. We expect miracles! The eternal law of sowing and reaping will not change as long as we remain on this earth. So, plant, grow, and use your faith! Your tiny, mustard seed faith will move any mountains standing in your way!

Faith requires action, so let's jump right into our next ingredient.

Ingredient #4
· Add Action ·

If you don't go after what you want, you'll never have it. "Lights, Camera, Action!" Yeah, I know this isn't a movie, but it's time to work and truthfully, I've just always wanted to say that. ☺

Did you think you weren't going to have to work? Did you think some goals, faith, and a why were enough? Who told you that lie? Being successful at anything requires work.

"What *does it* profit, my brethren, if someone says he has faith but does not have works? Can faith save him? ¹⁵ If a brother or sister is naked and destitute of daily food, ¹⁶ and one of you says to them, "Depart in peace, be warmed and filled," but you do not give them the things which are needed for the body, what *does it* profit? ¹⁷ Thus also faith by itself, if it does not have works, is dead." – James 2: 14-17 NKJV

Woah, here James says that unless faith produces action, it's dead. Faith without works is dead. So many people are wishing and waiting. But, without activity nothing will happen. Don't let your dreams die. Take action to achieve them. Nobody is going to do this for you. I read somewhere that life has no remote, you've got to get up and change the channel yourself. This is so true. So many people are waiting for some miracle to happen to them. But, we have the power to change our situation. We have the power to take control and taking control means getting busy. But, not just being busy for the sake of being busy. The actions you take must line up to your why.

Actions produce results. The right actions produce the right results. You don't get paid for having an idea. You get paid for making them happen. Become obsessed, that's the word lazy people use to describe the dedicated. But, make people think you're crazy. You know the truth though. It's them who are crazy for not running hard after their dreams. Why have people become so complacent?

Clear your mind of can't, because you can.

"I can do all things through Christ who strengthens me." – Philippians 4:13 NKJV

The Bible clearly tells us that we can do all things. It doesn't say some things, most things. It says ALL things. I wrote a poem several years ago as a reminder of this very thing.

<u>*Reminder*</u>

Philippians 4:13 is a reminder
That we need to take off our blinders
And see that we can do anything we put our minds to
Because through Christ, you have the ability to do
Anything. Anything. Anything.

Through. Christ. He's the key

Imagine what your life could be

There's no limit, not even the sky

And nothing beats a failure but a try

We can't fail because we believe in the One

Who gave us His only Son

And when He died for our sins

And three days later - with all power – He rose again

C'mon y'all that tells us that He loves us so very much

And He wants every single ounce of our trust

I recognize that some of us aren't there yet: we still doubt

But, as for me, without Jesus, couldn't live my life without

So...I dare you. I dare you to trust God with all your might

The battle isn't yours, it's His to fight

I dare you to dream the impossible dream

Some of y'all looking at me right now haven't a clue what I mean

Listen. Ephesians 3:20 tells us clearly

Through His power working in us merely

He is able to do... exceedingly... abundantly... above ALL that we can ask or think!

Did you hear me? Write the vision... Not in pencil, but in ink!

Stain the pages with your dreams
And believe that God will bless you out the seams

That's faith – knowing that He will
Miracles are happening today even still
Doesn't matter your position or how old you are
Your faith will take you so very far

So, again... Philippians 4:13 is a reminder
That we need to take off our blinders
And see that we can do anything we put our minds to
Because through Christ, you have the ability to do
Anything. Anything. Anything.

I hope you take heed to this reminder and take personal responsibility for your actions. Nobody owes you anything. If you're waiting for someone to come along and save you, I've got news for you. The only person who can change your life is YOU. God will send people to help you, but you must take responsibility for your own life.

"The only place success comes before work is in the dictionary." – Vincent Lombard

Ingredient #5
· Remove the Bad Seeds ·

Look through your dish of life. Who are you connected to?

Did you know that every time you subtract negative from your life, you make room for more positive? It's time to evaluate your associations. It's time to remove the bad seeds.

Make sure the people around you are doing you good and not harm. Get rid of stagnant friends and empty connections that lead to nowhere. Seriously, take a look at who's around you. If they aren't helping you grow, pouring into you, or helping you in some way, get rid of them. Use the "I love you, but..." method. These individuals will eventually drain you, so take heed. You can love them from a distance.

"Sometimes you have to move on without certain people. If they're meant to be in your life, they'll catch up." – Mandy Hale

Sometimes you have to move on without people. It's hard, I know. But, if they are meant to be in your life, they'll catch up. Don't wait for them. People don't grow at the same rate, at the same time. Don't put your dreams on hold waiting on other people. If you do, one day you'll wake up old, gray, wondering where life went. Cut the cord.

"Surround yourself with winners, big dreamers, big thinkers."

Associate with people that inspire you, people that will add to your growth, that will challenge you to new heights. Your destiny is too important to waste your time and energy on people who are sucking you dry. You are only going to be as good as the people you surround yourself with.

Don't be afraid to distance yourself. I realize that some of the most negative people in our lives can be those closest to us, our family and friends. I never said this was going to be an easy dish to make.

One of the biggest mistakes I've made in my life was letting people stay in my life much longer than they deserve. For my sanity, I've learned to love people from a distance. You'll need to do that too. But, first, I want you to forgive them for bringing unnecessary drama and negativity to your life. Then, forgive yourself for allowing it.

To advance in this next season, some people need to be removed. Everybody can't go where you're going.

"The question isn't who is going to let me; it's who is going to stop me." -Ayn Rand

Ingredient #6
· Focus ·

When energy is focused or concentrated, as through a magnifying glass, that light can set fire to paper. A laser beam can cut through steel because it's focus is intensified. Focus on your purpose. Focus on what matters most and push forward regardless of challenges, obstacles, and situations. Focus can beat the odds.

Having gained clarity about what it is you will be working toward and what we need to do to, it's time to focus.

To maintain a steady focus, you need to address the following three areas:

1. Focus on what's most important, not what's fun, easy and/or convenient.
2. Focus on one thing at a time, not on trying to multi-task.
3. Focus on the execution of an activity, not on the desired outcome.

We typically get distracted and sidetracked when we look too far forward and fill our heads with other thoughts or things that need to get done. However, when you focus on the execution of an activity you are unlikely to fall into this trap because all of your focus and attention is on what you're doing right now in the moment. This moment is all that matters. Everything else just fades away into the background.

This kind of focus is, of course, not easy. It requires discipline on your part to maintain your focus over the long-term.

Your future rests purely in your hands. **You and you alone can decide within each moment what you will focus on.**

> **"The successful warrior is the average man, with laser-like focus." -Bruce Lee**

Ingredient #7
· Discipline ·

Self-discipline to be exact. Out of everything, this may in fact be the hardest. You are going to want to take the easy way. We want to be comfortable. We want things to be easy. It's natural for us to prefer ease over hard. But, nothing grows inside of our comfort zones.

"If you don't design your own life plan, chances are you'll fall into someone else's plan. And guess what they have planned for you? Not much." -Jim Rohn

Discipline is one ingredient I really had a hard time with. As a child, I did what I was told. I was a good kid. At least, I hope I was. I tried hard not to cause my parent's grief, especially my mom. She had too many other things to worry about than little ol' me. So, I got good grades. I did my chores. I helped with the businesses. I stayed out of trouble. I followed the rules. Pretty much, I was quiet and my childhood went by without too much focus on me. Mission accomplished. Or, so I thought. When I became an adult, I went rogue. Well, as rogue as a Christian could be.

I was an adult and now that I was paying my bills and making my own way in this world, I didn't want to follow one rule that wasn't my own. I went to bed at 3am. I ate dessert for breakfast. I went to church when I felt like it. If I felt like it. I did what I wanted, when I wanted, with who I wanted.

Problem was, it wasn't healthy. That type of behavior isn't healthy spiritually, physically, or mentally. Now, we all want the freedom to live our lives the way we want. But, there are consequences to every action. How could I be a success without getting proper rest, eating right, or nourishing my spirit?

It's so hard to break bad habits. That's where personal development came in for me. But, even having the discipline to read every day became a challenging task. I started setting alarms to remind myself to read. Sometimes, books have great messages, but they can get a little boring. So, I started downloading the audio versions so I could do other tasks while simultaneously improving myself. It's amazing how learning a certain principle can apply to several different areas of your life. That's what happened for me.

For example, when I started reading about consistency (we'll talk about that in depth in a bit) in my business, I also applied the same principle to my healthy lifestyle goals. What if I hadn't been disciplined enough, not only to read personal development books, but also apply the information learned? I certainly wouldn't be a hundred pounds lighter, nor would you be reading this book.

Discipline for me, was learning how to remove temptations, avoid distractions, to prepare and plan, to set a routine, and to forgive myself quickly if I messed up. Nobody said we had to be perfect. The key is to keep moving forward, no matter what.

If you aren't currently developing yourself personally, you're doing yourself a great injustice. Get into the habit of reading EACH day. Yes, every single day you should be doing something to improve your life, your skills, your mind. I strive to do at least thirty minutes of personal development daily.

If you read 30 minutes a day with me, over the course of a week, that's 3.5 hours. An average sized book will approximately take you two weeks to finish. So, with 52 weeks in a year, you would end up reading about 25 books a year. Wowsers!

Don't you think that reading 25 books over the course of a year will change how you think about your life? Heck yeah it would! Your life would be transformed from learning from people all across the world who are willing to share their life lessons with you. You don't have to reinvent the wheel, you know. There are so many people who've traveled this same road to success. Let their failures and insights save you some time, energy, and money.

If you are not willing to learn, no one can help you. If you are determined to learn, no one can stop you. Learning and having discipline requires you to make certain choices. These choices aren't always fun. But, you have to force yourself to do what you should do no matter whether you like it or not. It's not about being an adult. It's about being a success. I hope you'll choose to discipline yourself enough to take personal development seriously. It is an empowering, life-changing habit that I've come to enjoy.

Ingredient #8
· Consistency ·

One of the most important lessons I learned this year is that consistency will make or break your dish. It is one of the most important ingredients to success. Consistency in thoughts AND actions. If you apply the principle of consistency to your life, you'll find it has the power to take you to the next level of success that you are seeking.

Consistency is one of the key things I teach to my network marketing team. Once they decide what their goals are and write them down, I help them work consistently to achieve them. We do something EVERY day to work towards those goals. This creates a habit and habits form actions and action leads to success.

"It's not what we do once in a while that shapes our lives. It's what we do consistently."
Anthony Robbins

Have you ever wondered how some people are able to achieve massive amounts of success in their field of endeavor, while others work just as hard but achieve very little? It's consistency.

To be consistent means to fully dedicate yourself completely to a task, activity or goal. It means to stay fully engaged without distraction.

Consistency is vital to success no matter what you are doing. No relationship can be successful without it. Human beings need consistency in love, hate, friendship, care, and every other human emotion. That is why when you are in a relationship, you would require your partner to be caring, loving, and faithful throughout the life time. If a partner fails in doing so, the relationship is seriously damaged.

Similarly, consistency in your professional life is also very important. If you are not consistent at work, you are not going to be successful. Consistent performance at work is the only thing that is going to get you positive reviews from your employer. These reviews are what gets you ahead in the company. That is why we see consistent people in the top positions or that have their own successful businesses.

Consistency establishes your reputation. If you're in business, growth requires a track record of success. You can't establish a track record if you are all over the place or constantly doing something different. Many efforts fail before they get where they see tangible results because of this very reason. Too often, the team simply didn't stay the course to achieve the goal. I've seen it time and time again.

Consistency maintains your message. No matter what business you're in, if you are leading people, you have a team. And, that team pays as much (if not more) attention to what you *do* as to what you *say*. You must be the example. This isn't "do as I say, not as I do" like some of us heard growing up. Lead by being consistent. They are watching and it serves as a model for how they will behave. If you treat a task or meeting as unimportant, don't be shocked when you find they are doing the same thing.

You and you alone are accountable for what you do and what you fail to do.

Now, if for any reason you feel that this is something that's tough to do, then consider for a moment all of the bad habits that you easily do without even realizing it.

For instance, snacking on chips, cookies, or overeating just a little each day over the course of many years can lead to weight gain and health issues. But, you probably won't notice what overeating "just a little" today is doing to you, because it really doesn't make much of a difference "today". It probably won't even make much difference tomorrow or next week, except for lack of energy. But, over time, overeating a little each day makes a significant difference. That is when you finally start seeing and REALLY feeling the results from your consistent daily actions. Consistency can go both ways. Be consistent with the right things. Make the right choices. When you do that, you are more likely to achieve your goals.

Now, many people struggle with consistency when they fail to see immediate results from their actions. I was one of the strugglers until I really got it. I wanted instant gratification, but it just doesn't work that way. If you are struggling too, you aren't alone. We live in a "microwave" society. We want everything right now. When we feel hungry, we order Chinese. When we get bored, we switch on cable television. When we get lonely, we chat online. All our lives, we've been programmed to expect that our desires will be instantly satisfied. However, when it comes to achieving our goals, the rules don't seem to apply. Why is that?

If you want to be successful, you need long-term vision and delayed gratification. You must consistently apply yourself over an extended period of time in order to reap long-term rewards. I know this isn't easy to do, but if you want true, long-term success, you'll do it.

Ingredient #9
· Stay Positive ·

My mother says all the time, "count it all joy!"

Our world has gone mad. I can't even look at the news anymore without cringing. It seems like there isn't any good news in the news!

So, how do we stay positive? Besides turning off the news? Well, we have to find sources of positivity and think on those things.

Count your blessings. Being thankful is a great way to focus on the good around you.

None of us can be relentlessly upbeat all the time, but a *positive* mind-set can be indispensable when the going gets tough. A negative mind will never give you a positive life.

In every day, there are 1,440 minutes. That means we have 1,440 daily opportunities to make a positive impact." – Les Brown

Stay positive. You can't stop the waves, but you can learn to surf. Your attitude is key to winning at life.

Have you ever heard the saying, "Your attitude determines your altitude?" Well, it's true.

"Attitude is a little thing that makes a big difference." Winston Churchill

Ingredient #10
· Never Give Up ·

Never, ever give up. It's not going to happen overnight and it's not supposed to. Great things take time. Nobody is an overnight success, even if it looks that way. Put in the work, be patient, dedicated, and consistent. It will all pay off.

"Therefore, my beloved brethren, be ye steadfast, unmovable, always abounding in the work of the Lord, forasmuch as ye know that your labour is not in vain in the Lord." – 1 Corinthians 15:58 KJV

Let nothing move you. Nothing. Be strong, knowing that what you're doing isn't useless, or in vain.

"Let us not grow weary in well doing, for in due time we will reap a harvest, if we do not give up." – Galatians 6:9 NIV

If we do not give up. If we do NOT give up. IF we do not give up.

Failure simply isn't an option. You must make the internal decision that you will never give up in the pursuit of fulfilling your dreams. Your goals must be backed up with determination and persistence.

Quitting isn't a way out. Quitting will lead you down a road where you'll never win. How can you win if you're not in the game? Stay in the game. Hold on. Don't let go, even when things seem uncertain or unclear. Just keep on going. Keep on keeping on!! Press through the many trials.

My father taught me how to persevere. I watched him fight many adversities. I saw and took pride in how he overcame obstacles and pushed his way through. He never finished high school, but he was brilliant. He never let no's, lack of money, lack of support, negative opinions, nothing sway him. If he had an idea, he ran with it. He hit roadblock after roadblock, and failed many times. But, he was the true definition of a winner. He knew he was different and didn't try to be like anyone else. He knew God placed something special in him. He knew he wasn't supposed to live a mediocre life and he knew he wasn't supposed to keep what he knew to himself. He also knew he couldn't give up.

A heart attack took him away from us on April 19, 2005, but his legacy lives on. Through me, my mother, my siblings, my nieces and nephews, each person he touched, and now you.

I believe that the longer you persist, the more you'll become convinced of your own greatness.

Ingredient #11
· Help Others ·

In society today, we look out for ourselves first, then we help others. That's good in some cases. For instance, during an emergency on an airplane. You put your oxygen mask on first, then you help your neighbor. But, when it comes to getting ahead, our thinking needs to change.

Zig Ziglar, one of my favorite motivational speakers once said, "You can have everything in life you want, if you will just help enough other people get what they want." **So, how do we help others?**

First, we need to stop being selfish and share information. We can't help everyone personally, but we can point them in the right direction. That includes your network. Plug people into other people who you believe will help them with their goals. Take the time to make personal introductions, too, whenever possible. You'll soon find that as you help someone expand their circle, your circle will also increase.

Second, show people the way. Be an inspiration to others by the way you live. Treat others with respect at all times. Never look down on anyone and show your appreciation for any job well done. If you lead a team, your example is everything.

They are watching you, even when you feel like they aren't.

Third, genuinely care about people. Pay close attention to their lives. Ask questions and get to know them. When you remember their children or another important detail, it lets people know that you care. The more people feel like you care, the more they will care about you. Never forget this: **People don't care how much you know until they know how much you care.**

These things aren't hard to do. You'll find these simple things will have a tremendous impact on your life, simply by focusing on others.

We've gone through every ingredient one by one. On the surface, it seems easy enough. But, it will take a strong WHY to make it through all the roadblocks you'll encounter. Success isn't a piece of cake. Get ready for the ride of your life. Here is the recipe again. Put these eleven ingredients to work and your life will never be the same.

Ingredients:

- 1 VISION
- 3 ¼ cups all-purpose WHY
- 5 large FOCUS
- 2 tablespoons BELIEF (100%)
- 1 pinch of FAITH (mustard seed size)
- 1 ½ teaspoon NEVER GIVE UP extract
- 3 cups SERVICE TO OTHERS
- 1 ½ cup ACTION
- 4 DISCIPLINE

- 1 dash CONSISTENCY
- Garnish: POSITIVITY

Directions:

1. Preheat your **Faith** to 350°. Beat *fear* at high speed with a heavy-duty **Vision** mixer until **Belief** occurs. Gradually add **Action**; beat at medium speed 3 to 5 minutes or until **Dedicated** and **Consistent**. **Remove Bad Seeds** and add 4 **Focus**, 1 at a time, beating just until **Vision** becomes clearer. After each addition, remember your **Why**. Stir in **Positivity** zest and **Discipline** extracts.

2. Add more **Action** to mixture, alternately with remaining **Focus**, beginning and ending with your **Why**. Beat at low speed until blended. Pour **Dreams** into a greased and floured *limitless* pan.

3. Bake at 350° for as long as it takes for your **Why** to become reality. Cool away from negative people.

4. Spoon **Helping Others** Glaze over warm or room temperature. Top **Success** with **Thankfulness** and **Giving Back**.

Conclusion

So, we have our goals, the reasons why we want to achieve them, and what to do to achieve them. We have a plan.

You can't change your destination overnight, but you can change your direction starting now.

You, of course, won't see much of a difference today, nor will you see much difference tomorrow, or even next week. But, by putting this recipe to work in your life, you will build the foundations of a far richer, happier and more fulfilling life. That, my friend, is success.

You are far more than capable of doing great things. You are. There will be people who don't want you to succeed. They will talk about you. They won't believe in you. They'll even try to hinder you. Oftentimes, these people will be your family and/or closest friends. But, you must know that there is a power inside of you greater than anything you could ever encounter. Tap into that power.

Much success to you... and, yours.

Notes

Recipes

Here are a few recipes that I think you'll enjoy. Share them with your family and friends. Celebrate your success! Bon Appétit!

Granny's Cornflake Chicken

Ingredients

- 4 pieces of chicken
- 3 cups of corn flakes
- Salt
- Pepper
- Poultry Seasonings
- 1 Egg
- 3 tablespoons melted butter

Instructions

❖ Preheat oven to 350 degrees. Take the skin off the chicken. Salt, pepper and put chicken poultry seasoning on breast front and back. Scramble egg in a bowl. Crush cornflakes and mix in butter and poultry seasoning (to taste). Dip breast into egg mixture and roll in the cornflake crust to coat. Mixture will be moist so you may have to pat it on there. Place them onto baking dish or aluminum foil. Bake for about 30 mins or until done.

Grandma Fonville's Hush Puppies

Ingredients

- 2c corn meal
- 2c boiling water
- 1 tbsp. bacon drippings
- 2 tsp baking powder

Instructions

❖ Mix corn meal, salt, and baking powder. Slowly beat in the 2 cups of boiling water, enough to make it sort of thick. Stir in the bacon drippings and shape into small balls of about 1 inch in diameter. Fry in deep fat until brown. Drain on paper towel and serve immediately.

Grandfather Charles' Meat Loaf

Ingredients

- 1 ½ lb. ground beef
- 1 can tomato soup
- ½ cup dry bread crumbs
- ¼ cup chopped onions
- 4 tsp. Worcestershire sauce
- 1 egg, beaten
- 1/8 tsp. pepper
- ¼ cup water

Instructions

❖ Mix together ½ cup soup, beef, crumbs, onion, 3 tsps. sauce, egg and pepper. Put in a 12 x 8-inch microwavable dish. Firmly shape into loaf and cover with wax paper. Microwave on high for 15 minutes or until firm in center (170 degrees). Rotate dish twice during cooking. Reserve 1 to 2 tablespoons of drippings. Let stand in bowl. Combine remaining soup, water, Worcestershire, and season drippings. Microwave on high for 1 minute. Makes six servings. For conventional oven: Bake at 350 degrees for 1 hour or until done.

Aunt Evelyn's Spoon Bread

Ingredients

- 1 1/4c milk
- ¾ tsp salt
- 3/4c yellow corn meal
- 1 can cream-style corn
- 2 tbsp. butter or margarine
- ¾ tsp baking powder
- 3 eggs

Instructions

❖ Scald milk and add salt, gradually stir in corn meal and cook over medium heat, stirring until thick. Remove from heat and stir corn and butter, then stir in baking powder and beat in eggs. Pour into buttered 2-quart casserole. Bake in preheated 375-degree oven for 35 minutes or until lightly browned and firmed. Serve with butter.

Aunt Alice's Broccoli Salad

Ingredients

- 1 large bunch of broccoli, finely chopped
- ½ cup raisins
- ¼ cup chopped onions
- 1 pound bacon
- 1 cup mayonnaise
- 2 tbsp. vinegar
- 1/3 cup sugar

Instructions

❖ Combine broccoli, bacon, raisins, and onion. Set aside. In another bowl, combine mayonnaise, sugar, and vinegar. Mix well and pour on broccoli mixture. Toss gently to mix well. Chill. Yield: 8 servings.

Aunt Joyce's Hot Rolls

Ingredients

- 7 cups of flour (all-purpose)
- ½ cup oil
- ¾ cup sugar
- 2 eggs
- 2 tsp salt
- 2 Rapid Rise yeast packets
- 2 cups milk

Instructions

❖ Scald milk, when lukewarm, add oil and sugar to milk. Stir well. Add to mixing bowl, then add flour, salt and well beaten eggs. Put yeast in small amount of warm water and tablespoon of sugar. When yeast rises, add to other mixture. Mix well with electric mixer. When well mixed, let stand until it doubles in size. Then place on baking sheet. After it rises, bake in 350 to 400-degree oven, until golden brown.

Mama Trina's Bread Pudding

Ingredients

- 6 c of bread, crumbled
- 3 c milk
- 2 eggs
- 1 tsp vanilla
- ½ tsp nutmeg
- ½ tsp cinnamon
- ¼ stick margarine
- ½ c raisins
- ½ c pineapple
- 1½ c sugar

Instructions

❖ Preheat oven to 350 degrees. Mix all ingredients together, except raisins, pineapple, and margarine on medium speed for 1 minute. Stir in raisins and pineapple. Melt margarine in pan. Pour ingredients in pan. Cook for 45 to 60 minutes until brown on top.

Grandma Fonville's Grated Sweet Potato Pudding

Ingredients

- 3 lb. sweet potatoes
- ¼ lb. softened butter
- ¼ c sugar
- ¼ tsp cinnamon
- ¼ tsp nutmeg
- ¼ tsp vanilla flavoring

Instructions

❖ Wash, peel, and finely grate sweet potatoes. Put into a large bowl and add softened butter and the rest of the ingredients. Put into a large buttered baking dish. Bake in a 375-degree oven for 1 hour, stirring often. Lower heat to 350 degrees and continue to bake until brown on top, approximately 45 minutes. This dish can also be cooked on top of the stove in a heavy skillet.

Lareesa's Pecan Sand Tarts

Ingredients

- 2 c butter
- 2 ½ c sugar
- 2 eggs
- 4 c sifted all-purpose flour
- 1 egg white, slightly beaten
- Pecans

Instructions

❖ Cream butter, add sugar gradually, beating until fluffy. Add eggs, one at a time, beating thoroughly after each addition. Add flour in fourths, mixing until well blended after each addition. Chill dough overnight. Remove from refrigerator only amount needed for a single rolling. Roll dough about 1/16-inch thick on a floured surface. Cut with 2-inch round or fancy cutter. Brush tops with egg white; sprinkle with a mixture of ½ c sugar and 2 teaspoons ground cinnamon. Transfer to ungreased cookie sheets and press a quarter of pecan on the center of each cookie. Bake at 350 degrees about 9 minutes.

Aunt Alice's Pound Cake

Ingredients

- 3 cups all-purpose flour
- 3 cups sugar
- 1 lb. butter
- ½ cup Crisco shortening
- ½ tsp salt
- ½ tsp baking powder
- 1 tsp lemon flavoring
- 1 tsp vanilla flavoring
- 1 cup milk
- 6 eggs

Instructions

❖ Let butter, eggs, Crisco and milk be room temperature. Grease and flour loaf pan. Cream butter and Crisco until smooth. Add sugar and mix well. Add one egg at a time, mixing well after each addition. Mix the flour, salt and baking powder together. Fold into cream mixture along with milk. Whip about 3 minutes. Add flavoring while whipping. Bake at 350 degrees for 1 ½ hours. Do not open oven for the first hour.

Aunt Gaynelle's Sweet Potato Biscuits

Ingredients

- 2 cups mashed sweet potatoes
- 2 ½ cups of Bisquick
- ¾ c milk
- 1 tsp cinnamon
- 1 tsp allspice
- 1 tsp nutmeg
- 1 tsp vanilla
- ½ cup sugar
- ½ cup butter
- 1 egg

Instructions

❖ Combine sugar, butter, egg, spices and vanilla to mashed sweet potatoes. Season to taste, then add to flour mixture. Roll out on floured cutting board about 2-inches thick. Cut out and put on greased cookie sheet. Set oven to 450 degrees and bake about 15 minutes or until done. Remove from oven and brush with melted butter. Serve hot.

I hope you enjoy these comfort foods, in moderation of course! Please be mindful of the following when planning healthy meals for you and your family:

Proteins: Support growth and maintain body tissue. It also regulates the balance of body fluids and helps in the production of antibodies. Sources include eggs, meat, and cheese, some breads, cereals, dried beans and peas.

Carbohydrates: Carbs are the body's main source of energy. Without them, the body relies on fat and protein as sources of energy. Sugars (fruits and sweets) and starches (vegetables, pasta, and bread) supply carbohydrates.

Fats: To support and protect internal organs, a certain amount of fat is necessary. Fatty meats, some cheeses, and nuts are sources of fats.

What to watch out for:

Saturated Fats: Some scientists believe that a high-fat diet plays a role in high blood pressure, so be sure to watch your saturated fat intake. When your blood pressure rises, you put yourself at risk of suffering a heart attack.

Cholesterol: Cholesterol is essential to many of the body's chemical processes. It is manufactured by the body and stored in the liver, and comes from the food we eat. However, too much cholesterol thickens your arteries. Foods high in cholesterol are whole milk, cheeses, yogurt, sour cream, egg yolks, ice cream, butter, and organ meats, like liver. Be heart smart and watch your cholesterol intake.

What should you eat?

Eat more fruits, vegetables, and whole grains. Eat fewer high-fat foods. Eat fewer foods rich in refined sugars. Eat fewer foods rich in sodium. Eat in moderation.

One thing that I try to do is incorporate more vegetables into my diet. For the longest time, I didn't eat many vegetables or only ate certain ones. But, now I realize, vegetables aren't only good for you, they are simply good!! Especially, when prepared right. So, here's a beginner's guide to proper vegetable preparation times:

If you're new to the kitchen or trying to shake things up a little, it's helpful to know which vegetables cook in a similar manner. Of course, you can use a wide variety of cooking methods (steam, grill, roast, sauté) and the size of the vegetable will further determine the cooking time. In general, if you're trying out a new vegetable, go ahead and buy up a big bag at the farmers' market and try cooking it a few different ways until you find the one best for you.

For the sake of comparison, the following guide assumes boiling.

Cooks Quickly (5 minutes or less)
- Asparagus
- Broccoli
- Carrots
- Corn
- Eggplant
- Green Beans
- Mushrooms
- Peas
- Spinach

Cooks in 10 to 15 minutes
- Brussels Sprouts
- Cauliflower
- Squash

Just Keep Cooking (15 minutes+)
- Artichokes
- Beets
- Collard Greens and other hearty greens
- Potatoes

Tips:
• Cook vegetables until soft, but so they still have a bite to them (think green beans that remain firm rather than droopy).
• To keep vegetables from overcooking before serving, submerge in ice water to stop from cooking and again briefly in boiling water when you're ready to serve.

Now that we have cooking times down, we need to make sure we are using seasonings that really enhance our dishes. Here's a complete guide:

Dried Herbs & Spices

- **Asafoetida (Asafetida)** - Used as a digestive aid in Indian cooking. It has a strong odor, but that mellows out into a nice garlic-onion flavor.
- **Achiote Paste and Powder** - Reddish-brown paste or powder ground from annatto seeds with an earthy flavor. Used primarily in Mexican dishes like mole sauce and tamales.
- **Allspice** - Similar to cloves, but more pungent and deeply flavored. Best used in spice mixes.
- **Annatto Seeds** - A very tough reddish-brown seed with a woodsy aroma and an earthy flavor. Called Achiote Paste when ground, this is used to flavor many Mexican dishes.
- **Bay Leaf** - Adds a woodsy background note to soups and sauces.
- **Caraway Seed** - These seeds are commonly used for soda bread, sauerkraut, and potato salad.
- **Cardamom** - This warm, aromatic spice is widely used in Indian cuisine. It's also great in baked goods when used in combination with spices like clove and cinnamon.
- **Cayenne Pepper** – One of my favorite spices to use. It's made from dried and ground red chili peppers. Adds a sweet heat to soups, braises, and spice mixes.
- **Chia Seeds** - No, these seeds aren't just for growing crazy sculptures! Nearly flavorless, they can be ground into smoothies, cereals, and baked goods for extra nutrition and texture, or even used as a vegan egg substitute.

- **Cinnamon** – I love cinnamon! Found in almost every world cuisine, cinnamon serves double duty as spice in both sweet and savory dishes.
- **Cloves** - Sweet and warming spice. Used most often in baking, but also good with braised meat.
- **Coriander Seed** - Earthy, lemony flavor. Used in a lot of Mexican and Indian dishes.
- **Cumin** - Smoky and earthy. Used in a lot of Southwestern U.S. and Mexican cuisine, as well as North African, Middle Eastern, and Indian.
- **Fennel Seed** - Lightly sweet and licorice flavored. It's excellent with meat dishes, or even chewed on its own as a breath freshener and digestion aid!
- **Fenugreek** - Although this herb smells like maple syrup while cooking, it has a rather bitter, burnt sugar flavor. Found in a lot of Indian and Middle Eastern dishes.
- **Garlic Powder** - Garlic powder is made from dehydrated garlic cloves and can be used to give dishes a sweeter, softer garlic flavor.
- **Ginger** - Ground ginger is made from dehydrated fresh ginger and has a spicy, zesty bite.
- **Gochugaru** - This Korean red pepper spice is hot, sweet, and slightly smoky.
- **Grains of Paradise** - These tastes like a cross between cardamom, citrus, and black pepper. They add a warming note to many African dishes.

- **Kaffir Lime Leaves** - Used to flavor curries and many Thai dishes. Can be sold fresh, dry, or frozen.
- **Loomi** - Also called black lime, this is ground from dried limes. Adds a sour kick to many Middle Eastern dishes.
- **Mace** - From the same plant as nutmeg, but tastes more subtle and delicate. Great in savory dishes, especially stews and homemade sausages.
- **Mahlab** - Ground from sour cherry pits, this spice has a nutty and somewhat sour flavor. It's used in a lot of sweet breads throughout the Middle East.
- **Nutmeg** - Sweet and pungent. Great in baked goods, but also adds a warm note to savory dishes.
- **Nutritional Yeast** - Very different from bread yeast, this can be sprinkled onto or into sauces, pastas, and other dishes to add a nutty, cheesy, savory flavor.
- **Oregano** - Robust, somewhat lemony flavor. Used in a lot of Mexican and Mediterranean dishes.
- **Paprika** - Adds a sweet note and a red color. Used in stews, spice blends, and great on deviled eggs!
- **Peppercorns** - Peppercorns come in a variety of colors (black, white, pink, and green being the most popular). These are pungent and pack a mild heat.
- **Rosemary** - Strong and piney. Great with eggs, beans, and potatoes, as well as grilled meats.

- **Saffron** - Saffron has a subtle but distinct floral flavor and aroma, and it also gives foods a bright yellow color.
- **Sage** - Pine-like flavor, with more lemon and eucalyptus than rosemary. Found in a lot of Italian cooking.
- **Smoked Paprika** - Adds sweet smokiness to dishes, as well as a red color.
- **Star Anise** - Whole star anise can be used to add a sweet licorice flavor to sauces and soups.
- **Sumac** - Zingy and lemony, sumac is a Middle Eastern spice that's great in marinades and spice rubs.
- **Turmeric** - Sometimes used more for its yellow color than its flavor, turmeric has a mild woodsy flavor. Can be used in place of saffron in a pinch or for those of us on a budget.
- **Thyme** - Adds a pungent, woodsy flavor. Great as an all-purpose seasoning.
- **Vietnamese Cassia Cinnamon** - Sweet and spicy. Can be used in both sweet baked goods and to add depth to savory dishes.

Fresh Herbs

- **Basil** - Highly aromatic with a robust licorice flavor. Excellent in pesto, as a finishing touch on pasta dishes, or stuffed into sandwiches.
- **Chervil** - Delicate anise flavor. Great raw in salads or as a finishing garnish.
- **Chives** - Delicate onion flavor, great as a garnish.
- **Cilantro** - From the coriander plant, cilantro leaves and stems have a pungent flavor. Used in Caribbean, Latin American, and Asian cooking.
- **Curry Leaves** - These pungent leaves are not related to curry powder but impart a similar flavor. Used in Indian, Malaysian, Sri Lankan, Singaporean, and Pakistani cuisine. Used to flavor curries, soups, stews, and chutneys.
- **Dill** - Light and feathery herb with a pungent herb flavor. Use it for pickling, with fish, and over potatoes.
- **Lemon Thyme** - Sweet lemon aroma and a fresh lemony-herbal flavor. This is excellent with poultry and in vinaigrettes.
- **Lovage** - Tastes like a cross between celery and parsley. Great with seafood or to flavor stocks and soups.
- **Marjoram** - Floral and woodsy. Try it in sauces, vinaigrettes, and marinades.
- **Mint** - Surprisingly versatile for such an intensely flavored herb. Try it paired with lamb, peas, potatoes, and of course, with chocolate!

- **Oregano** - Robust, with a subtle lemon flavor. Used in a lot of Mexican and Mediterranean dishes.
- **Parsley** - this very popular herb is light and grassy in flavor.
- **Pink Pepper** - Small and sweet, these berries are fantastic when marinated with olives or simply sprinkled on bread.
- **Rosemary** - Strong pine flavor. Great with eggs, beans, and potatoes, as well as grilled meats.
- **Sage** - Pine-like flavor, with more lemon and eucalyptus than rosemary. Found in a lot of Italian cooking.
- **Summer Savory** - Peppery flavor like thyme. Mostly used in roasted meat dishes and stuffing, but also goes well with beans.
- **Shiso** - A member of the mint family, this herb is used extensively in Japanese, Korean, and Southeast Asian cooking as a wrap for steaming fish and vegetables, in soups, and as a general seasoning.
- **Tarragon** - Strong anise flavor. Can be eaten raw in salads or used to flavor tomato dishes, chicken, seafood, or eggs.
- **Thai Basil** - A spicy, edgier cousin to sweet Italian basil. A must-have for Thai stir-fries, Vietnamese pho, spring rolls, and other South Asian dishes.
- **Thyme** - Adds a pungent, woodsy flavor. Great as an all-purpose seasoning.

Measurements Conversion Chart

US Dry Volume Measurements

MEASURE	EQUIVALENT
1/16 tsp	dash
1/8 tsp	a pinch
3 tsp	1 Tablespoon
1/8 cup	2 tablespoons (= 1 standard coffee scoop)
1/4 cup	4 Tablespoons
1/3 cup	5 Tablespoons plus 1 teaspoon
1/2 cup	8 Tablespoons
3/4 cup	12 Tablespoons
1 cup	16 Tablespoons
1 Pound	16 ounces

US Liquid Volume Measurements

8 Fluid ounces	1 Cup
1 Pint	2 Cups (= 16 fluid ounces)
1 Quart	2 Pints (= 4 cups)
1 Gallon	4 Quarts (= 16 cups)

About the Author

Lareesa Fonville is a business advisor, mentor, and entrepreneur. She enjoys helping others dig deep and find the motivation inside themselves to create a successful life. She believes everyone already has 99% of what it takes to be successful. She helps them find the 1% that's left.

If you enjoyed this book, please do the author the favor of leaving a review on Amazon. Thank you in advance.

Contact Us

We'd love to hear from you!

REEcipe For Success
P.O. Box 35893
North Chesterfield, VA 23235

Email: lareesainc@aol.com
Web: http://www.lareesa.com

Connect with me: @lareesainc